anything

Public Transportation

LET'S RIDE THE
STREETCAR!

Elisa Peters

press.

New York

Published in 2015 by The Rosen Publishing Group, Inc.
29 East 21st Street, New York, NY 10010

First Edition

Editor: Amelie von Zumbusch
Photo Research: Katie Stryker
Book Design: Andrew Povolny

Photo Credits: Cover TFoxFoto/Shutterstock.com; p. 5 Jorg Hackemann/Shutterstock.com; p. 6 Steve Frame/Shutterstock.com; p. 9 James Mattil/Shutterstock.com; pp. 10, 14 iStock/Thinkstock; p. 13 Paul Todd/Gallo Images/Getty Images; p. 17 GVictoria/Shutterstock.com; p. 18 John Hester Photography/Shutterstock.com; p. 21 Bruce Leighty/Photolibrary/Getty Images; p. 22 Svetlana Bekyarova Photography/Flickr/Getty Images.

Publisher Cataloging Data

Peters, Elisa.
Let's ride the streetcar! / by Elisa Peters — first edition.
 p. cm. — (Public transportation)
Includes index.
ISBN 978-1-4777-6518-0 (library binding) — ISBN 978-1-4777-6523-4 (pbk.) —
ISBN 978-1-4777-6513-5 (6-pack)
1. Street-railroads — Juvenile literature. I. Peters, Elisa. II. Title.
TF148.P4818 2015
625.6—d23

Manufactured in the United States of America

CPSIA Compliance Information: WS14PK4: For Further Information contact Rosen Publishing, New York, New York at 1-800-237-9932

CONTENTS

Streetcars are a good way to get around cities. They run on **rails** in the street.

MAIN
STREET
ONLY

DANGER
HIGH
VOLTAGE

They are also called trolleys. In England, people call them trams.

They have motors. They draw power from a **wire**.

9

A trolley pole links the streetcar to the wire.

The driver is called a **motorman**. He controls how much power the motor gets.

Melbourne is in Australia. It has the longest streetcar network.

Toronto is in Canada. It has a big network, too. About 275,000 people use it each day.

510

4193

STOP
behind open
streetcars
doors
IT'S THE
LAW!

DO NOT PASS
OPEN DOORS

STOP

STOP

東方飯子樓

FAMOUS
CANADA
INC.

香島西餅

Some cities use modern cars.
New Orleans uses old-style cars.

The Fox River Trolley Museum is in South Elgin, Illinois. It is fun to visit.

SHORE LINE ROUTE
EVANSTON

715

It is fun to ride a streetcar. Have you ever been on one?

WORDS TO KNOW

motorman

rails

wire

WEBSITES

Due to the changing nature of Internet links, PowerKids Press has developed an online list of websites related to the subject of this book. This site is updated regularly. Please use this link to access the list:
www.powerkidslinks.com/putr/stcr

INDEX

C
cities, 4, 19

M
motor(s), 8, 12

N
network, 15–16

P
power, 8, 12

W
wire, 8, 11